Positive Thinking

Changing Your Mind-Set Can Help You Achieve Happiness And Success In Life; Put An End To Negative Thoughts

(Efficient Manual For Swift Personal Growth And Immediate Happiness)

Patrick Runge

TABLE OF CONTENT

Cognitive Behavioural Therapy: What Is It?............... 1

Methods Of Positive Thinking... 9

Fruitful Partnerships..25

Entering The Present..50

The Influence Of Hope 71

Putting More Fuel In Your Internal Fire......................88

Positive Thoughts And The Attraction Law...........108

Cognitive Behavioural Therapy: What Is It?

The term Cognitive Behavioural Therapy essentially describes a type of limited-session systematic psychotherapy or mental health counseling. You and a mental health counselor—a therapist or psychotherapist—participated in these sessions. Thought patterns and learn how to respond more effectively to difficult circumstances to produce positive outcomes.

Depression and anxiety are only two examples of the many mental diseases or disorders that can be treated with cognitive behavioral therapy. However, while everyone can benefit from cognitive behavioral therapy, this does not imply that only those with mental illnesses can. Everybody encounters stressful situations daily, and everyone could benefit from cognitive behavioral therapy to learn better coping mechanisms.

Cognitive behavioral therapy addresses a range of emotional problems. This therapy can be used with other therapies, such as medicine, or alone to manage the symptoms.

If you suffer from a mental disease, you may experience relapses. Such a relapse may be avoided with the help of this therapy.

Cognitive Behavioural Therapy becomes the ideal alternative if you have a mental condition but are unable to take medication (for example, because you are pregnant).

If all you want is advice on handling the different stressful circumstances that arise in life, Cognitive Behavioural Therapy is another option. For instance, you might face issues in your marriage or at work that you are unsure how to handle. This therapy will help you understand how to handle those circumstances.

Anger is one of the many emotions we experience but often don't know how to deal with. You will learn how to control your emotions during this therapy.

You may improve your communication skills and learn how to handle conflict in relationships with cognitive behavioral therapy.

This therapy will teach you coping mechanisms for situations where you lose a loved one.

Cognitive behavioral therapy is something you should think about if you have ever gone through any form of emotional trauma related to abuse or violence. It will help you deal with the trauma.

This therapy is beneficial for managing a variety of mental health conditions, including chronic fatigue syndrome and cancer.

This therapy can help manage chronic physical symptoms such as fatigue, pain, and insomnia. You should try it if you have any of these symptoms.

When someone receives Cognitive Behavioural Therapy, several mental health issues can become better, including:

Disorders related to anxiety

diseases of the personality

problems of sleep

OCD, or obsessive-compulsive disorders

Psychosis

Sexual dysfunctions

Fears

Bipolar illnesses

PTSD, or post-traumatic stress disorder

The best results from Cognitive Behavioural Therapy are sometimes obtained with other therapies, such as antidepressants or medicines.

Chapter 4: Recognising and Replacing Limiting Beliefs to Overcome Negative Thought Patterns

These self-limiting ideas might prevent us from realizing our full potential since they are frequently the result of social indoctrination, self-doubt, or traumatic events. This chapter will provide techniques for recognizing these harmful thinking patterns and swapping them out with empowered, uplifting ideas.

Identify and Accept Negative Thoughts: Being conscious of one's negative thought patterns is the first step towards conquering them. Keep an eye on your inner monologue and deliberately try to recognize any self-defeating or negative thoughts that surface.

Face Your Limiting Thoughts: It's critical to challenge the validity of your negative thought patterns once you've recognized them. Consider if these ideas are founded on knowledge or are just presumptions and anxieties. You can start to break these thoughts' grip on your thinking by confronting them.

Use Positive Affirmations to Replace Negative Thoughts: Positive affirmations must replace negative thoughts if you want to change your thinking. These affirmations should challenge your limiting beliefs with precise, grounded, empowering truths. If you frequently tell yourself, "I'm not good enough," try telling yourself, "I am capable and deserving of success."

Visualise Success: Overcoming unfavorable thought patterns can be accomplished using visualization. Shut your eyes and visualize yourself reaching your objectives, feeling happy, and reaping the rewards of your success. Practice Mindfulness and Self-Compassion: Mindfulness exercises, like emotions, make recognizing and changing negative thought patterns easier. This mental imagery can help to rewire your brain and reinforce positive thought patterns. You can also release limiting ideas by cultivating a more understanding and forgiving relationship with oneself through self-compassion practice.

Be in a Positive Environment: Your mental processes can be greatly influenced by the things around you. You may assist in reinforcing a positive mindset and combat negative thought patterns by surrounding yourself with positive influences, such as encouraging friends, literature, and media.

Establish Achievable Goals: Overcoming negative thought patterns can be facilitated by setting realistic, attainable goals that will help you gain confidence and self-esteem. You will start to notice proof as you accomplish each objective, evidence that both validates your positive thinking and refutes your limiting beliefs.

Seek Professional Assistance If Needed: After discovering that your negative thought patterns are extremely distressing or deeply embedded, you should seek assistance. They can offer direction, encouragement, and strategies to help you eliminate limiting ideas and adopt a more optimistic outlook.

A key component of harnessing the power of positive thinking is breaking free from negative thought habits. You can start changing your thinking and realizing your full potential by recognizing your limiting ideas and replacing them with thoughts that will empower you. Recall that developing positive thinking is a continuous process that calls for perseverance, self-compassion, and deliberate effort. As you continue, you'll reap the transformative powers of an optimistic outlook.

Methods Of Positive Thinking

A positive outlook can be developed by individuals using a range of positive thinking approaches or practices.

Here are a few examples of common optimistic thought patterns:

1. Optimism: Two traits of optimistic thinking are expecting the best and searching for the best under the given conditions. It emphasizes keeping a positive outlook and trusting that everything will work out for the best. Positive people usually see setbacks. Positive people usually see setbacks as isolated and temporary events rather than widespread or permanent.

2. Gratitude: Gratitude-based positive thinking is acknowledging and celebrating life's blessings. It strongly emphasizes being thankful for the good things, people, and events in life. Gratitude is a technique that can help redirect attention from problems or challenges to the abundance and blessings already there.

3. Self-affirmation: Reiterating one's value, competence, and good traits through the intentional and purposeful use of helpful language is known as self-affirmation. It can help with confidence building and getting rid of self-defeating beliefs. "I am capable," "I deserve love and happiness," or "I have the strength to overcome obstacles" are a few examples of affirmations.

4. Reframing: This tactic involves consciously changing one's perspective or understanding of a situation. It is taking on new, positive perspectives and focusing on the lessons or chances from a difficult or bad event. Reframing facilitates the shift in perspective from one of victimization to one of initiative and empowerment.

5. Positive Self-Talk: Positive self-talk involves replacing negative or self-defeating words with positive and inspiring ones. It entails being kind and supportive of oneself in inner dialogue and

ideas. Constructive self-talk can boost motivation, resilience, and self-worth.

6. Visualisation: Creating vivid mental images of desired outcomes or satisfying experiences is the art of visualization. It involves seeing oneself reaching goals, overcoming obstacles, or discovering contentment and happiness. Behavior that is driven, self-assured, and goal-directed is enhanced by visualization.

7. Mindfulness: A crucial element of mindfulness is living fully in the present moment without passing judgment. It entails accepting ideas, emotions, and sensations but remaining indifferent. People can overcome negative thought patterns and their experiences by practicing mindfulness.

It's critical to realize that these techniques for positive thinking are not exclusive of one another and that integrating and mixing many ideologies can be beneficial for individuals. Proactive actions and problem-solving should go hand in hand with positive thinking to create lasting change in one's life.

Day 1: Gratitude practice and positive intention setting

We are embarking on a life-changing adventure to develop optimistic thinking today. As you begin this 14-day program, pause to make a plan for the days that lie ahead. Think about how your thoughts affect your world and their strength. You can access opportunities and personal development when you intentionally select positive thoughts.

Put your good intentions for the following two weeks on paper. These could be upbeat affirmations, objectives, or aspirations. Allow them to strike a deep chord with you and act as your compass during this program. Whether you aim to "I choose to focus on the good in every situation" or "I am grateful for the abundance in my life," let it inspire and motivate you.

Pause to acknowledge the blessings and happy times in your life. List three things for which you are thankful today. They could be large or small, material or immaterial. It might be the flavor of a mouthwatering meal, a loved one laughing, or the sun's warmth on your cheek.

Allow yourself to experience the full range of feelings connected to these moments as you write down your thankfulness. Allow appreciation to seep into every part of your being, giving you a feeling of satisfaction and appreciation. Never forget that appreciation may be found in even the little things; it is not just reserved for large gestures or noteworthy occasions.

Being grateful makes us feel better and helps us think positively. It assists us in changing our attention from what is missing in our lives to what is abundant. Regularly engaging in acts of thankfulness may teach our minds to find the good in any circumstance, even when things are difficult.

Make it a challenge for yourself to remain grateful all day long today. When pessimism threatens to intrude, deliberately shift your focus to the things you are thankful for. As blessings come to mind, jot them down and compile a growing list. You may establish a strong foundation for positive thinking by grounding yourself in appreciation.

As this program ends, consider your goals and the expressions of thanks you have shared. Accept the feeling of hope and opportunity that permeates your soul. Building on the groundwork we set today, we will resume our path toward positive thinking tomorrow. Have faith in the procedure, have confidence in yourself, and let optimism lead the way.

Day 2: SELF-REFLECTION AND POSITIVE AFFIRMATIONS

Greetings on Day 2 of the 14-day course on optimistic thinking!

Today, we'll go into more detail about the effectiveness of self-reflection and positive affirmations. Repeating affirmations to yourself helps you reframe your thoughts and strengthen empowering beliefs. They can change your perceptions, which in turn changes your reality.

Make a note of the affirmations that positively speak to you. These declarations should represent the values, principles, and aspirations you hope to uphold. Conviction and intention are key when writing affirmations like "I am capable of achieving great things" or "I radiate love and positivity." Remember that these statements can change the way you view yourself.

After you've listed your affirmations, let's discuss self-reflection. Reflecting on oneself involves taking stock of your feelings, ideas, and actions. You can learn more about your patterns, beliefs, and potential growth areas. Through developing self-awareness, you can actively select constructive ideas and deeds.

Give yourself some time to consider your feelings and ideas. Do you have any limiting ideas or bad tendencies that prevent you from adopting positive thinking? Acknowledging their existence in your life, put them in writing. Next, confront and transform these ideas into empowering and constructive ones. If you constantly tell yourself, "I'm not good enough," change your mindset.

It's crucial to approach yourself with kindness and compassion when you reflect on yourself. Realize who you are and realize that you are a work in progress. Recall that everyone occasionally feels self-conscious and has bad ideas. The secret is to identify, confront, and swap them out for empowering statements.

Consider your self-talk as you go about your day today. Observe any negative or counterproductive thoughts that come to mind. When you see yourself thinking negatively, stop and deliberately replace those ideas with encouraging statements from your list. Let them permeate your subconscious mind by repeating them with belief and commitment.

Although self-reflection and positive affirmations are effective techniques, they need regular application and practice. Throughout the day, deliberately work on repeating your positive affirmations. These can be silently repeated in your thoughts during times of quiet reflection.

Recall that positive affirmations can build positive thinking muscles and reprogram your brain. They assist you in developing a strong, positive outlook. Recognize that every affirmation is a step towards a happier and more satisfying existence, so embrace this practice wholeheartedly. As Day 2 of the program ends, pause to acknowledge your progress. Recognize how effective self-analysis and positive affirmations can be in changing your perspective. As we proceed to positive thinking, we will discuss the significance of surrounding yourself with positive influences tomorrow. Continue your fantastic effort!

Section 1: Grasping the Idea of Positive Thought

When motivational speakers assert that "you have to think positively to achieve any form of success," what does it mean? Does this imply that you must see the world in rainbow colors? Does this imply that you should overlook the incorrect things and less enjoyable circumstances in life and stick your head in the sand? Not!

Thinking positively does not mean ignoring the challenges we face in life or our flaws. It has nothing to do with fabricating a reality.

Positive Thinking: What Is It?

Selecting to view life's challenges and the negative aspects of yourself in a more constructive and upbeat manner is known as positive thinking. Even if things might not seem good right now, you hope for the best rather than the worst. You don't run away from or disregard the bad things. But you decide to take advantage of them and bring out the best in them.

For example, when a romantic relationship ends, consider the possibility that your partner left because they could not recognize the special beauty in you rather than because they thought you were not pretty or lovable enough. This will give you the impression that you are lovable and haven't met someone who finds you attractive, which will help you move on.

An optimist chooses to think positively, whereas a pessimist chooses to think adversely.

While an optimist acknowledges that the glass is not full, he or she ignores the empty space and interprets the glass as half full. A pessimist, on the other hand, will only see emptiness and refuse to acknowledge the contents of the glass. The key to positive thinking is in your explanation of your experiences. A positive explanation approach characterizes optimistic thinkers. When something positive happens, they take credit for it. When events beyond their control go awry, they assign responsibility to other entities. They also see difficult circumstances as abnormal and transient.

Pessimists and negative thinkers don't give themselves enough credit for their accomplishments. When you congratulate someone on a success, they may feel you are making light of them or pulling their leg. Additionally, they see bad things as inevitable and permanent; one of their frequent refrains is, "I knew it would happen like this."

You will never be at peace if you expect awful things to happen and continually blame yourself for events beyond your control. Ultimately, thinking negatively might affect your mental health and reduce your quality of life.

Thinking positively is deliberate and logical.

Abraham Lincoln once said, "Most people are about as happy as they make up their minds to be."

As the reasons above may have suggested, even in the face of adversity, you should think positively to be happy. Thinking positively is incorrect because it teaches us to "look the other way"—ignoring reason and convention in favor of optimism. Although it is wrong, nobody wants to be miserable. Thus, the only useful, desirable, and legitimate method of thinking remains positive, which ensures you will live a happy life. It makes sense to choose optimistic thinking. Optimistic self-talk encourages optimistic thinking. Let's study more about encouraging self-talk.

Positivity in Thought and Self-Talk

Positive self-talk stems from positive thinking. Self-talk can also refer to the never-ending flow of unsaid ideas that cross your head every second. It need not be the words you say out loud to yourself. According to studies, people have between 50,000 and 70,000 ideas every day. Approximately 70% of such thoughts are deemed to be negative, according to Psychology Today. More than 90% of those ideas are automatic. Furthermore, our minds frequently forget about happy thoughts instead of unpleasant ones.

Where is the source of self-talk?

These ideas may arise from your reasoning and logic. Culture—what society has held to be true ever since humans were able to reason—and the false beliefs you make due to ignorance when you don't know any better are two more sources.

For example, being thin is the new beauty in today's world; if you don't fit the definition of thin, many find you ugly. Every day, films, TV series, and other media present this to us. Many of us, regrettably, struggle to reach those "perfect sizes," and when we don't manage to drop a dress size, we begin to believe things like "I am so fat and ugly." The current quo influences this negative self-talk. Positive self-talk provides you hope when you tell yourself things like, "I am fat, I am beautiful, but I will get on a diet and work out to improve my physical fitness."

Your mental state, level of productivity, and overall health are all impacted by how you talk to yourself, which is influenced by how you think. You may tell yourself positive and uplifting things you would tell a loved one, so you must program your mind to think optimistically. A proverb goes, "Your beliefs become your thoughts, which become your actions, which then become your reality."

Some psychologists believe that while optimistic thinking can lead someone to take unwarranted risks, realistic thinking is preferable. Though it is the only way to think positively and experience good things in life, as was previously noted, thinking positive thoughts is ultimately not "right." With more experience, you'll be able to reduce the number of "unrealistic" thoughts and limit yourself to only those that will improve your life.

Let's talk about why you should adopt positive thinking instead of any other now that we clearly understand what it is.

Chapter 3: The Advantages of Positivity

Wellbeing

The tension that negative thinking causes is bad for your health. It is detrimental to both your physical and mental wellbeing.

Most people are unaware that stress can be linked to even seemingly unimportant things, like being overweight. We all know, of course, that some people, but the cortisol released during. Therefore, thinking positively will benefit you far more than thinking negatively, regardless of how much your health or the size of your swimsuit matters to you.

Fruitful Partnerships

Your bad self-perception or negative attitudes towards other people are the root of the problem, making it difficult for you to sustain connections and forcing you to stay in unhealthy partnerships that you should absolutely end.

More fruitful relationships are always the result of thinking positively, projecting a positive image of yourself, and giving others a chance rather than always viewing them negatively.

Hope Is Never Lost

Since positive thinking is typically more accurate than negative thinking, it is preferable. The next time you're tempted to label yourself an idiot, keep that in mind. No, you're not a moron. Either you made a mistake (great! You know what not to do the next time), or you didn't know something, which is great! You have something new to learn. Are any of those statements untrue? No, not at all. However, do you typically consider them in times of need? That's right. And there is the issue.

The fact is that hope never goes away. Recall that those questioned have always been on the wrong side of history. Now, those who denied that humans would ever reach the moon appear ridiculous, and those who never imagined that humans would ever fly at all look almost completely mad. Those who only highlight the impossibility are never going to make it happen. However, those who affirm that they are correct. They leave their mark on the world and lead far happier lives, so I wonder how we can do it. It will not help you to overcome the odds of thinking negatively.

Taking the Self-Fulfilling Prophecies by Surprise

The term' self-fulfilling prophesy' is typically employed to discuss situations in which individuals had self-doubt and ultimately failed due to those doubts. The problem is that if the self-fulfilling prophecy is true in the negative, it may also be true in the positive.

What if you believe in your ability to overcome obstacles you never would have expected to overcome? What if you put aside your misgivings and try doing the seemingly impossible rather than just watching the earth spin and the time run out? It used to be impossible to fly. It was also impossible to abolish slavery. It used to be impossible to be in the same room with people sitting in Turkey, Australia, England, Canada, and Mexico simultaneously—we could only go to the moon and cure the plague—but people manage to do it daily in online chat rooms.

By estimating the risks but not allowing them to deter you, having faith in the possibilities and yourself... Perhaps there is nothing you can do. But you will undoubtedly fail to do anything if you think you can't. If you focus only on the obstacles, you ensure that those will be your only challenges and that they will always put an end to you. Why? Because you weren't prepared to accept that you would ever succeed, and you already assumed they would.

How do we quit thinking negatively when it's a waste of time? Before it stops us, how can we stop it?

Chapter 2: Mindfulness Practices for a More Contented Life

Our outlook determines how we live. Our lives will seem to be one long, unbearable misery without hope if we give in to the negativity connected to our suffering and those we witness around us through friends and the media. We gradually develop a habit of thinking negatively and believing life is awful.

But suppose we deliberately work to think positively, to be upbeat, and to avoid letting obstacles get in the way of our goals. Eventually, our lives will start to look nice, and the negativity will just go away.

An established and widely accepted belief on habits states that anything you consistently perform for 21 days will eventually become ingrained in your life. Similarly, practice positive thinking by sticking to the routines listed in this chapter for at least 21 days, and you'll see a noticeable improvement in the quality and happiness of your life.

Maintain a thankfulness journal. When we experience one negative occurrence in a day, we tend to forget all the positive things that occurred before and after that one negative event. Make it a daily habit to list five positive things that have happened in your life. When you identify things in your life to be thankful for, you'll notice a shift in your mood. Show gratitude! It is the starting point for discovering optimism.

Embracing gratitude offers the following advantages:

increases your feeling of contentment

provides long-lasting satisfaction

keeps stress and negativity at bay

lessens your reliance on worldly possessions

increases the fulfillment of your relationships

Stress reduction promotes relaxation and improved sleep.

Accept failures: You must learn to accept rejection, failure, defeat, and other setbacks as inevitable aspects of life. These are ephemeral, constantly shifting occurrences. You don't succeed today; someone else does. You pass tomorrow; someone else fails. As you grow from the mistakes of your failures, you become stronger and gain more expertise in handling hard situations. Remember the old phrase, "Failure is the stepping stone to success."

Use upbeat and joyful language to explain the happenings in your life. You might be surprised to learn how much our word choices influence our lives. How you view your life will determine how it turns out. You see your life this way, believing it to be hectic, monotonous, chaotic, and uninteresting. These hurtful remarks will have an impact on both your body and mind. However, if you speak with adjectives like energetic, cheerful, content, and full of vigor, you will truly experience these happy things.

Take a look at the following statements and try changing the wording to see the magic that can happen in your life:

I have laundry to pick up.

I have to put in a lot of effort.

I have bills to pay.

I have to give my kid food.

Now consider the following sentences:

I got to take the clothes out.

I got to work hard.

I can settle the bills.

I get to feed my kid.

When you switch out "have" for "get," your perspective on life completely shifts. The word "get" conveys a sense of thankfulness, whereas "have" turns the task into an obligation you must perform. Putting forth a lot of effort at work provides your family with food, shelter, and enough money to meet their needs and fulfill your own. Transform the events in your life from chores you have to do to opportunities you are thankful for.

Don't let the negative attitudes of others drag you down; you've been having a terrific day, are satisfied with the results of your work, and are eager to return home to a supportive family. Suddenly, a coworker of yours enters your office and begins to whine about something that, up until that point, didn't seem like a problem at all.

Eventually, you become tired of hearing the other person whine all the time, and you unintentionally start agreeing with what he or she has to say. Before you know it, your wonderful day is gone. When you get home, life is miserable, and you are irritable, bitter, and angry.

Acknowledge these occurrences in your life and remember to ignore or keep such people's yelling voices far away. Don't let the whiny attitude of others affect you unnecessarily.

When issues are being discussed, try to find solutions. Being optimistic does not require you to lose awareness of issues. Conversely, your optimistic approach to the issues will facilitate the resolution of the problems. By approaching difficulties and issues objectively, positive thinking helps you view the world realistically and be free from the emotional baggage that comes with it. There will be answers. Therefore, when individuals share their difficulties, they try to find solutions rather than correcting them.

Make someone smile at least once by asking yourself, "Who do I think of the most? That's going to be you. We consider ourselves, our issues, ways to address them, ways to prevent them, ways to go about living this life, ways to live that life, etc. Whether we realize it or not, we are the center of our universe. Every day, attempt to bring joy to someone else. We become acutely aware of how much potential we have to positively influence the world around us when we consider the pleasure of others. This gives you more self-assurance and happiness.

Look for positive things happening in the world—violence, hatred, wars, and battles are all too often. News of deaths and devastation, sometimes natural but more frequently man-made, abounds in the media. However, these depressing tales are interspersed with many tales of bravery and kindness. Concentrating on these tales will increase your sense of optimism and joy, and your nagging sense of skepticism will vanish.

When we have a bad attitude, it keeps us from being joyful and makes other people around us unhappy. Therefore, put in the extra effort to be upbeat and think positively. With persistent effort, you will eventually find that this attitude becomes a habit you cannot break!

Section Two

Negative Feelings Will Result From Negative Thoughts

Feelings come from thoughts; feelings cannot exist without thoughts. Consider how you think when you are stressed or concerned, for instance. You will be thinking of worried ideas. Take a stab at this experiment. Flip through a magazine and utilize the photographs to assist you in shifting your perspective rather than just taking a quick look at them. When you see a photo of a contented youngster, attempt to put yourself in the child's shoes and think like the child for a little while. Next, look at another image, and while you gaze at it, imagine certain feelings that go with it. This demonstrates that external cues can cause emotions to be triggered. A picture of anything horrifying could make you feel afraid on the inside. That's a typical reaction. You must, therefore, learn how to regulate your emotions in various circumstances. Instead of believing that the issue is insurmountable, you must be able to take a step back and identify answers. When a parent receives an issue from a child, the parent is presumed capable of solving it, which may take some time. The same skill needs to be taught to your conscious mind. Remind yourself that everything has an answer rather than taking the problem at face value right away. Move on from the issue, and the positive information you gave your subconscious about the likelihood of a solution will assist it in finding one rather than allowing negativity to consume it.

Having a pessimistic outlook on life will only result in suffering.

Have you ever met someone you thought was exhausting and noticed they appeared to attract bad luck? If so, you've probably noticed that we avoid unpleasant people like these because we don't want to absorb their negative, toxic, and depleting energy. You ought to stay away from certain people in your life. These are the poisonous individuals who not only bring negativity into your life but also make it miserable for you. When you think of that person, you will know that the pessimism they share with you will always taint your thoughts when you come into contact with them. This means that you are creating the opposite of a people magnet, which is why people will avoid you if you start to feel dissatisfied and have a bad outlook.

Lonely people frequently feel lonely due to their thoughts and occasionally even how they make other people feel. Observe the contented individuals. They seem to be able to ward against pessimism better than others who would rather dwell in it, and they attract joyful people. You will eventually become one of those positive people if you practice becoming like them.

When anxiety, fear, and doubt consume your thoughts, you lack the will to accomplish your objectives. Your mindset is holding you back if you want to start a new career or lose weight. You don't have the confidence to take the first step because you believe it will be too difficult. You then begin to feel even more depressed as you haven't made any progress. It's also unclear how you think in this way. Your head is so full of useless ideas that you become mentally tired, which can result in tension and burnout. If you are so entrenched in this mindset, how can you hope to attain prosperity and well-being?

Numerous health issues are caused by unhealthy thinking and a pessimistic perspective. To help you comprehend, let us demonstrate a common case.

Kate is experiencing dyspepsia. An ache shoots through her chest. The ache intensifies as she informs her thoughts that her heart is acting strangely. She feels so sick that she lies down. She only experiences heartburn as a result of eating her meals too rapidly. She lies on the bed, and as her anxiety increases, her blood pressure rises as well, causing her to become hyperventilated. This indicates that she is breathing heavily and is taking in too much oxygen, which is why you are perspiring. Kate might have addressed all her issues in the manner listed below without suffering any unfavorable consequences.

Kate is experiencing dyspepsia. She is aware that she ate her meal too quickly. She consumes an indigestion medicine, tells herself she needs to learn to eat more slowly, and carries on with her day.

The second case scenario differs from the first in that Kate learned from her error and applied it to her future endeavors. She refrained from indulging her fears and anxieties. She gave it some advice for the future. Instead of attempting to find answers, Kate, in the first case scenario, made matters worse by exaggerating the nature of the issue.

Practice self-control

Examine yourself the next time you see a worried, irate, afraid, or nervous thought slipping in. Seek a favorable reaction from it and proceed. Consider what you can learn from the circumstance and what it could be attempting to teach you. You will discover that by making issues seem bigger than they truly are, you let yourself get agitated. When you do this practice, you will stop building mountains out of molehills instead of letting negative thoughts creep into your mind. Learning the advantages of training your mind to think in solutions rather than problems can cause you to think very differently and enable you to do things you never would have believed you were capable of. Give up, undermining your prospects of happiness. Make regular use of this technique to start seeing life differently.

Establish both short- and long-term goals (Insight #5)

The incapacity to create both short- and long-term goals is a characteristic shared by most dissatisfied and unsuccessful people. Let's explore goal-setting, how to set it, and how it relates to achieving success and happiness.

The connection between happiness and goal-setting

You can't have a feeling of direction in life if you don't make goals. You have no idea what steps you need to take or what goals you must reach to succeed in life. This gives you no hope, and you become sad when you have no hope left. On the other hand, you can look forward by establishing goals. You have hope for a better tomorrow because you know what you want out of life, and when hope enters your life, happiness begins to flow.

Furthermore, you never remain inert once you begin to set goals. Instead, achieving your goals motivates you to advance, seize new chances, and reap the rewards of success, all of which contribute to your pleasure. Therefore, you must begin creating goals for yourself to achieve actual happiness.

Establishing Goals

This is not at all a tough step. To achieve your goals, all you have to do is identify what your greatest lifelong want is. You already know your true desire if you have done the activity covered in the first chapter. The next step is to develop your lifetime goal or goals while keeping that want, wish, or dream in mind. One of your ultimate life goals could be to become a well-known songwriter and perhaps even a vocalist if music is your love and you hope to become a successful songwriter. While it is possible to have multiple lifelong goals, most are related. For example, your long-term objectives can be to start your own music business, get wealthy, and become a successful vocalist. These objectives are all connected. But you can also have other long-term objectives.

Setting short-term goals is the next step you need to take after determining your ultimate aims. Essentially, the short-term objectives are subsets of the long-term objectives. The long-term goals appear challenging to attain since they are projected over an extended period. Your long-term goals must be divided into smaller, more achievable, and controllable objectives, known as short-term ones, for you to get closer to them. Determine the necessary measures to reach your long-term objective; these will serve as your short-term targets. If you dedicate yourself to putting them into practice and take decisive action, you will soon discover that you are getting much closer to your ultimate goals, making you feel accomplished and content.

Take Lessons From Your Suffering

Admit your errors and learn from them to avoid repeating the same ones.

What role am I performing in this? Keep in mind that you are not the victim. Recognize your role so that you can adjust it. Live with the mindset of empowerment. Being a victim means you relinquish power to "others."

Stop thinking like a victim instead of viewing your circumstances as a reflection of who you are within. A victim mindset may become apparent to us because of pain. Being a victim confines you and gives you no power. Thus, it's critical to recognize and overcome this mindset. Reclaim your authority.

Past experiences are one source of emotion, especially the emotion of pain. This is significant since recognizing the incident or incidents and the feelings they arouse in you is the first step towards altering this dynamic.

A study revealed that feelings arise before you can analyze the event that triggered them. This is because your subconscious mind generates the emotion, and your conscious mind takes longer to understand it. Thus, we think after we have felt. That is a sobering realization. But as you'll see, knowing this will give you power.

When you experience negative emotions such as pain, anger, doubt, impotence, or inferiority, it's because your subconscious mind connects the recent occurrence to a similar past event, which is why you feel the same way you did at the time of the original event.

There may be more than one source of the pain. Your conscious mind may be unable to comprehend why the current event triggered the unfavorable feeling. Your conscious mind searches for an external cause. This is akin to adopting a victim attitude, as we cannot change an external source.

The real source of the feeling is inside. Events are neutral in theory, so internal factors must be at play. Think about this. When ten people go through the same thing, you receive ten distinct emotions—some of which are comparable. Every one of the ten individuals uses a unique collection of life experiences to attribute feelings to that specific incident.

You carry these unpleasant feelings within you as a component of your worldview. Pain is useful because it indicates the harm already inside you, and once you know where the damage is, you may start to repair it.

The current incident will enhance the pain response to similar situations if the damage is not repaired. If you do not address the harm, you will keep drawing individuals and circumstances that make you feel bad. Thank goodness for these unpleasant feelings, without which we would not be able to identify the harm and take action to fix it.

The individuals we care about and have drawn into our lives—those closest to us—frequently participate in these painful occurrences. Most people we love and who love us don't mean any harm. They don't intend to cause you harm. If they are, then this is not the case, and you ought to give your relationships some thought. Apart from that, though, there's a good chance the thing or someone that made you feel bad wasn't meant to harm you.

Think about this instance. A middle-aged, overweight man signs up for a gym and works out for the first time. He shows up with a big beer belly and love handles covered by a white t-shirt. He makes his way to the weight machines, where he spots a close friend who has lately put on muscle and dropped weight, lifting far more than he can now. At that moment, the man has feelings of impotence and inferiority since he thinks his friend is stronger than him and that he is unable to raise the same amount of weight. His feelings aren't coming from the friend in the gym. The root of the problem is internal. Even if his friends want to support him and have good intentions, there are bad feelings.

Entering The Present

Events can occur at any point in your life and cause your environment to become disoriented. You tend to dwell on all the bad things that have transpired when this occurs. A child loses confidence when their best buddy passes away since they no longer have someone they can rely on. We are powerless over the events that occur throughout our lives. Suppose you are anxious about an interview and feel unqualified. In that case, it's likely because your mental processes are telling you that you are unqualified, and you believe them rather than because you are insufficient. Confident and cheerful people give off a different vibration than those who approach situations in life with pessimism. Interviewers and others alike will notice this.

I've known people who have shown me how negative energy depletes your energy and leaves you feeling exhausted. I recall thinking that I was doing things for other people to try and obtain approval and that I didn't even really like them in those friendships that I had that offered nothing to my life. We are all guilty of this, and I'm sure you can name at least one individual that drains your vitality. That is what you do to people when you are negative. It's not benefiting you well as a result. You don't need their approval because you are who you are, and their affirmation won't change anything. So, the second approach is to help you let go of your need to know what other people think of you and instead learn to live in the present moment.

It's acceptable if you don't feel like doing yoga; nonetheless, one of the practice's tenets is learning to live in the present. It's a helpful method to lift your spirits and put you in a happier frame of mind. The method for doing this is rather easy. You just put away the negative thoughts you caught yourself thinking and focus only on the senses—touch, sight, hearing, smell, and taste. Live in the now. Take a look at yourself and begin to focus your thoughts on your life right now. Do the skies appear gray or blue? Is there a lovely scent? Why not, if not? Include one. The issue, as you can see, is that your life is going by without you experiencing it.

Let's make this simpler. Your mind will be in the past if that is where you are always thinking. It won't be soaking up the sun or indulging in the aroma of that amazing beverage in your hands. It is not going to notice the seasons or the amazing things that are visible in the garden. It will come to a standstill. Take advantage of this unique moment to bring optimism into your life, and watch as everything transforms.

I can see cobwebs on the bushes outside the window, left by spiders who worked through the night, as I write these words here. The sun glinting against the dewdrops caught in the cobwebs gives the impression of a lovely diamond necklace. But if I hadn't learned to live in the present, I would have simply gone about my day without realizing that opportunities for growth and development are always present in life and are available to everyone who wishes to seek them out.

A taste of your favorite cuisine could reveal your power. It may be sensed in a June wind. You might even taste it at a time when life's beauty leaves you speechless or hear it in your favorite piece of music. You lose all those chances if you're not in the present. Feel the cup's warmth against your fingers as you hold it up. Take in the scent. Instead of gulping the beverage down as quickly as possible, taste it and allow it to slowly coat your tongue. This allows your entire senses to fully appreciate the experience.

You will discover that you may create a calm and contented existence if you apply this strategy each time life appears overwhelming. Your senses are meant for just that, and as you develop their use, you'll find yourself inspired to take greater pleasure in life.

Section Two

The Impact of Pessimistic Thoughts

Has the proverb "mind over matter" ever occurred to you? Its basic idea emphasizes the influence of our thoughts on how we respond to and manage any given circumstance, regardless of whether it involves feelings of pain, fear, weakness, or something else entirely. However, its meaning may vary according to the individual.

This proverb also applies to mental control since it tells us that we always control how we will respond to any given stimulus.

At the close of the last chapter, we were reminded that thinking bad thoughts would not make them come true. This is an accepted reality. Our entire being is significantly impacted by the strong tool that is our mind.

Your thoughts will determine what you do in any given circumstance. For instance, you might drop your briefcase and spread your files across the hallway when someone bumps into you. A pessimistic person will probably start to yell, their blood pressure will likely rise over normal, and they might even start a fight with the individual who unintentionally bumped them. I'm going to be late. I might have misplaced some vital papers, and such thoughts will take over. Following the encounter, you'll feel like a cloud is hanging over your head, and negativity will mar you all day. Negative thinkers will either lose it or their day will spiral out of control due to the previous circumstance.

A positive thinker would probably accept the apologies, pick up the papers, and carry on with their day as if nothing had happened. Do you notice the difference?

Though it goes deeper than that, you could assume that this is just about a bad day. Your bad thoughts have taken control of your identity, emotions, interpersonal relationships, physical and mental well-being, and even yourself.

The "nocebo" effect, sometimes known as the placebo effect's evil twin, is another consequence of negative thinking in the medical industry. The scenario that follows will demonstrate just how strong our thoughts can be. A patient was diagnosed with a deadly condition, with only a 40% chance of survival, but with appropriate care, the patient could recover. Doctors often try to present a detailed picture of your health status, but depending on how that information is conveyed or perceived, it may have unfavorable effects. A pessimistic patient will choose to accept the 60%

likelihood of death rather than clinging to the 40% chance of survival. The patient has the option to refuse any recommended treatment or to proceed with it in a dejected manner rather than receiving the appropriate care. You know the potential consequences for those who lose their will to live. And here it is once more—the mind's power. You can persuade yourself to dwell on your sorrows and eventually pass away.

The following are some consequences of negative thinking that will cause you to reevaluate your thoughts:

Physical well-being: It has been demonstrated that our ideas are connected to various facets of our existence, including our physical well-being. Our thoughts impact our emotions and feelings, which might lead to health issues. Hopelessness and depression are examples of unpleasant feelings that result from negative thoughts and can throw off the hormonal balance in our bodies and even deplete the chemicals in our brains that make us happy. This will negatively impact Your immune system, which will weaken your defenses.

Lowered energy and endurance can also be caused by negative thinking.

Poorly controlled thoughts that lead to repressed rage, including digestive problems, hypertension, and cardiovascular diseases.

When our mind is overflowing with unfavorable ideas and perceptions, our body will create dangerous cortisol and adrenaline levels.

Recent research indicates that emotional patterns may also be linked to some disorders. Our mental habits also influence these patterns. Eliminating unfavorable thoughts from your head is the first step in reaching your ideal state of health if you care about your health.

Emotional downhill: Anger, worry, irritation, impatience, and other bad emotions are brought on by negative thinking. We are positive that these feelings must be resolved because allowing them to persist can lead to more serious issues like depression.

Unfavorable social environment: You influence others via your ideas, feelings, and behaviors. When thinking badly, we give out a certain energy to other people. Keep in mind that your words and deeds might arise from your ideas. You might become aloof, combative, or even afraid of other people.

The law of attraction states that we cannot draw in good things that could assist us in escaping unpleasant circumstances when we think negatively. Our mental states draw unfavorable feelings and even situations. This is the idea behind the Law of Attraction, which states that your focus will bring about the things you want in your life. You should anticipate unpleasant things happening if you dwell on the negative. This will probably happen to you if you believe you will fail and face hardship. Your unfavorablemindset will impact your self-assurance, output, and other success-related factors. Your thoughts become a reality. Similar people are drawn to your thoughts, even though you may be unaware of them. It is very unlikely that two pessimistic thinkers will form a positive relationship. If you dwell on the negative, tension and anxieties will become your closest companions.

Restricting your options: Let's say your boss assigns you a project, and because of the time limits, it makes you feel stressed out and unhappy. You will quickly realize that you wasted time and energy worrying rather than starting since you constantly worry that you won't be able to complete the tasks on your list. When you have pessimistic thoughts, your brain narrows down your alternatives for approaching tasks or any other scenario. You concentrate on your worry and dread of failing. Ultimately, what you are afraid of is genuine.

Time wastage: By thinking badly and allowing the gloomy feelings that go along with it to consume you, you are wasting time. If you can see the bright side of things, why be negative? When you can just be joyful, why waste your time being sad, angry, or depressed? You are aware of the detrimental impacts that negative thinking has on your relationships with people, your emotions, and your health. Therefore, you know you need to change right away. Keeping an optimistic outlook on life is always a better option.

If you are a negative thinker in general, how would you know? The following are indicators that someone is a negative thinker, per the Mayo Clinic:

● Filtering: You decide to draw attention to a bad part of the circumstance and leave out all the positive aspects. As an illustration, let's say you wrote a fantastic piece but included a few typos. You tend to focus on your mistakes and overlook the excellent aspects of your post rather than the aspects that others find admirable.

● Personalizing: You are probably aware of this one: you tend to take responsibility for negative things that happen to you. If your lover were to cheat on you, for instance, you would immediately place the blame and believe that you are the reason the relationship did not work out rather than admitting that you are a victim.

● Catastrophizing: This will resonate with you if you are a persistent worrier. Rather than hoping for the best, you prepare for the worst. Since your thoughts determine your mood and actions, if something unpleasant happens to you at the beginning of the day, you will begin to believe that the remainder of the day will be terrible as well, which is likely to happen.

● Polarizing: You limit things to two extremes, good and horrible. For instance, you can think an event you planned was fantastic or a complete bust. There are no "it went smoothly, or it went okay" ideas, and if you label it as a failure, you'll be hard on yourself for not being flawless.

You can tell that a change has to be made if any of those four signs apply to you. You now understand the detrimental consequences of having a pessimistic outlook, which can significantly impact how your life unfolds. Would you like to keep reaping those negative consequences? Or would you rather make a difference in your life and take the right course? I hope the upcoming chapter will persuade you to take more constructive action.

Chapter 5: The Influence of Your Environment on Your Thought Process

The most familiar object in our surroundings is our surroundings; this includes the meals we eat and the relationships we hold in the highest regard. Occasionally, the same things we find relatable can play a detrimental role.

I think the main reason for poor emotional setbacks is certain stressful environments. Some people may become so accustomed to stress in their surroundings that they lose sight of the advantages of positive thinking. You can be in a similar circumstance, where the toxic nature of your surroundings prevents you from seeing anything but bad things. But the result you have to work for will matter more in the long run.

I was speaking with my coworkerAa few weeks ago. W., who was narrating to me how he had overcome depression. A.W. and his family relocated from Puerto Rico to the United States a few years ago. They used to reside in the most impoverished area of the city, where drug lords and gang violence were commonplace. As the eldest of two children, A.W.'s parents were not wealthy. Had to work to support his parents financially after school. A.W. adored fast food and would visit his preferred neighborhood diner after work. After some time, he gained some weight, which led to bullying at school and a decline in his confidence. Furthermore, because his family doesn't have much money, A.W. and his siblings were prohibited from participating in after-school activities. He started to feel alone because of this.

A.W. thought there was no hope and that his world was dark. In his perspective, only successful people achieved their success via sheer luck. His mother would remark things like, "This environment is not what makes you, but creates something great," A.W., even though she attempted to encourage good behavior. Continued to view his surroundings as unfavorable and nothing more. Following the difficult divorce of his parents, A.W. began to decline significantly. A.W. went into a depressive episode. He began to run afoul of the school rules and nearly left.

About a year later, things began to go south when A.W. and his pals attempted to take over a car, which resulted in his spending several months in juvenile jail. Finally, A.W., having learned from his mistakes, ultimately sought counseling and treatment. A.W. went on to graduate from college, adopted new eating habits, developed new acquaintances, and began attending seminars that promoted virtue. These days, he attempts to inspire people to think optimistically by giving speeches at neighborhood gatherings.

Even though A.W.'s tale can be somewhat related to it, he lived in a very negative atmosphere. Does the world around you shape who you are? Just as long as you let it. This is the tale of a man who, by only separating himself from some of the bad influences and objects in his environment, was able to overcome his depression.

The Influence of Beginning the Day in a Positive State

The fact that you wake up every day is a good thing! You can take pleasure in life and the surroundings in your special ways. You have a fresh opportunity to come across inspiring and upbeat individuals or fantastic situations that will make a big difference in your life!

For many, it may be sufficient to start with that thinking, but there are additional things you may do when you get up that would be beneficial. In the same way eating a hearty, healthy breakfast is usually considered advantageous, it might be just as crucial to actively participate in activities that will feed your intellect. These include reading, avoiding unfavorable information, visualizing or utilizing affirmations, and exercising.

Some recommend reading books that focus on personal growth or have an upbeat tone when reading. This could also add links to publications or quotes that are helpful.

As far as possible, you should try to minimize the amount of unpleasant information you are exposed to in the morning. For instance, avoiding social media first thing in the morning could be beneficial for some people because there are often critical articles or comments there.

Others would make similar suggestions regarding the newspaper or the daily news on television (or radio). News articles often provide useful information but frequently discuss catastrophes and other ideas that some people would find offensive.

Remember that there are always good reasons to stay informed about the state of the world and your specific area, so this is not advice to fully cut off or shun news. But take note of the stories' tones and try not to allow yourself to become agitated, bitter, anxious, or pessimistic.

A wonderful way to start your day is to work out! Exercise can be either mental or physical, or both. Starting their days with a jog, walk, or run might be the best option for some folks. You can admire the world's beauty or reflect on the good things in your life while exercising this way, which also helps increase blood flow. People who exercise regularly report feeling more positive and confident about themselves generally.

Mental workouts can be anything from brainteasers like crossword puzzles to daily trivia questions and, as previously noted, reading upbeat materials to push oneself to think more optimistically. As you'll see in a moment, visualization, affirmations, and meditation are crucial mental activities.

Exercise Suggestion: The following day, attempt to start your day without being exposed to news coverage. As you begin your new day, think about short-checking the news while getting mental exercise or reading uplifting items.

The Influence Of Hope

Many would try to downplay or dilute the importance of positivity, writing it off as merely a mental attitude that wouldn't stay in a person's life permanently. It could seem weird to someone who has grown too accustomed to viewing things negatively. However, you'll find that having an optimistic outlook on life will offer you an advantage over any challenges. It is the element that separates success from failure. Optimism can help you accomplish your objectives and get through all the duties regardless of the outcome. Check out a few actions below to inspire you to view your life more enthusiastically and positively.

Get inspired now.

We frequently look to others around us for inspiration. Holding them responsible for the results of a task. When our goals are not achieved, it is simple to place the blame elsewhere, yet motivation should always come from the inside. That could be easier said than done, particularly if you tend to think negatively. So, what is your method?

Moving is the first step towards becoming motivated. Move in a literal sense. Do something to get your blood flowing in the morning, like pushups, jogging, or stretching. It would create a sense of enthusiasm in your head and prepare you for the remainder of the day when you are physically ready. Get ideas from others and view films about people who had humble beginnings but overcame adversity with faith and tenacity.

You have to start small, just like those people who are successful. We frequently find ourselves unable to finish the goals we have set for ourselves in the midst of them. Instead of taking on a lot at once and never finishing anything, starting and finishing one modest work is preferable. When you witness these little chores being finished one at a time, you'll discover that your motivation levels increase.

Announce your aim to the world as one way to boost motivation. Post your monthly weight loss goal, for instance, on the timelines of your close friends and family to hold them accountable for your progress. Your feet would be glued to the treadmill if you knew that your loved ones were tracking every step you took and providing you with affirmations.

Recall your accomplishments.

The idea that you must examine your history to go forward may seem weird, but it is accurate and useful. Your past successes are the one thing you can look back on with nostalgia. This would undoubtedly motivate you to overcome any obstacles you may be encountering. You may find the methods you've previously employed to accomplish a task and adapt them to your present assignments. Engage in a meaningful discussion with those who have supported you throughout the years and receive their advice on how you overcame a particular challenge in the past. These individuals possess distinct perspectives regarding your personality that you might have overlooked previously. Assigning value to your present aim would be much simpler if you could provide substantial evidence of your past achievements.

Get Rid of Distractions

When your mind is always racing with ideas, it might be challenging to concentrate on one task at a time. Your mind betrays you, and your thoughts wander as quickly as you want to concentrate on a subject. Your mind seems unable to manage all the thoughts racing through your head, making you feel defeated and pessimistic.

Recognize your unique approach to conquering obstacles and take control of your thoughts. Go ahead and pump up the volume if you need music to focus. However, if the music is distracting you, find a quiet place to work where you can remove outside distractions from your thoughts. Another option is to attempt verifying your routine and conduct again. Having social media open in your browser while attempting to complete work will entice you to check your feed and completely sidetrack you from your objective. If so, log off from all social media platforms while working.

Furthermore, technology is the largest hindrance to accomplishing specific objectives. No matter how determined you are to finish a task, it can divert you. It's important to remember that technology should govern you, not vice versa. Technology may help you accomplish your goals more quickly and effectively if utilized properly.

Have a competitive mindset.

Healthy competition is one of the most important things in achieving any objective. Positive competition would encourage you to demonstrate previously denied abilities and strengthen your assertiveness. Being competitive without being hateful or greedy will make you an achiever. Viewing obstacles and problems positively would be simpler if you consistently trust yourself when taking on a task. There will come a time when you will welcome obstacles and eagerly anticipate addressing them.

Never hesitate to seek assistance.

Building trust with those around you is one of the qualities a person should have. Keep in mind that it's acceptable to feel weak occasionally, particularly when anxiety strikes. When trustworthy individuals surround you, it will be simpler to seek assistance when your head is still filled with unfavorable ideas. While trying to think positively is a healthy thing, there are situations in which worrying causes anxiety severe enough to warrant medical care. If this occurs, contact someone qualified to deal with the most severe form of pessimism.

You'll be able to take charge of your ideas once you master the power of optimism. It would be hard for you to face a task and not feel confident that you can overcome it once you have mastered all these ideas and attempted to incorporate them into your daily life. A major component of happiness in this otherwise self-centered environment is optimism. Let's continue to the following chapter to discover further methods for achieving your desired happiness.

Chapter 5: Work on Mental Strengthening, Step #4

Increasing your memory to retain more information is one method of mental strengthening. Making the best selections will always be difficult if you fail to remember crucial details about a circumstance or problem. Possessing outstanding cognitive and memory abilities will benefit your personal and professional life. Here are some efficient methods for improving memory to help you with your next task.

Take an Emotional Interest in the Procedure

Emotionally charged events are typically easier for us to recall than dull ones. According to research, you seem to recall more when your emotions are high. Recall a period when you made a mistake despite your best efforts to impress your supervisor. You felt you had let the company and your boss down, as he was unhappy. You likely promised yourself that you wouldn't make the same error twice. You will always remember your error and take every precaution to avoid it since you are highly emotionally invested in your profession and want to present the best version of yourself and your boss to others. Renowned speaker, educator, and preacher Eric Thomas claims that finding your WHY will motivate you to take action. His motivation stems from a painful event he went through with his family. He says in his talks that he would not be as accomplished and motivated as he is now without the experience. Your capacity to establish meaningful connections with the circumstances will determine how much more you can recall. This, in turn, depends on how quickly you can take in information and store it in your long-term memory.

Your emotional connection to the material you are trying to learn and remember is one of the things that drives this process. When you want to properly recall something, pay attention to it and concentrate on each stage of the procedure. Visualize the event in your mind to further involve your subconscious in the process and the information. This makes for powerful memories that you can quickly access when necessary, and those recollections will motivate you to act.

Indian industrialist Ratan Tata is worth a billion dollars. He asserts that a person should possess the mental fortitude necessary to meet obstacles. You can make difficult and dangerous decisions because of your mental toughness. Ratan once worked aimlessly for eight years of his life without understanding what his ultimate purpose was. Looking back on his life, he believes those eight years taught him far more than he could have imagined. You may occasionally discover that you are acting without understanding why you do it a certain way. You should have the mental fortitude and the necessary faith to make important judgments during those times. Your mental toughness greatly influences your capacity for action. As you age, You'll understand that not everyone you know shares your objectives and aspirations. You will feel loneliness at some point in your life, whether you are currently experiencing it or not. You won't be alone, not because you won't have somebody to spend time with or converse with, but because you will notice that those around you don't share your mindset. This is where the idea presented in Chapter 4 enters the picture: You require a positive environment around you. You will have to make decisions for yourself as you become older. When choosing friends and associates, Ratan advises, "You should do what you believe is right." Following your convictions is one of the hardest and riskiest decisions you will ever make. You'll need the mental fortitude to handle it; you could even start to doubt yourself, but if you follow your convictions, you'll succeed. You won't look back on it, at the absolute least.

Handling Unforgiveness

Today's psychology claims that regrets are bad for your body and mind. I once told Rick, one of my coworkers, that I would leave the company to follow my passions. Rick would be retiring in five years. He told me a personal story as I was nearing the end of my stay. When Rick was a youngster, his father founded a business. Sadly, Rick's father could not keep up with the business due to personal and financial problems. Consequently, he was forced to close the business. Rick once asked his father if he regretted choosing to launch a business. Do you know what his father's reaction was? He wanted to continue, but he regretted stopping it. He did not regret starting one. Rick continued living his life after the death of his father, replaying this discussion in his mind constantly. He got busy taking care of his family after having them. Guess what he regrets now that he is five years away from retirement? Rick said, "I should have tried." When you consider everything you have regretted in your life, it's more likely that you regret what you chose not to do than how you handled a particular situation. Your mental fortitude becomes weaker the more regrets you have. Get rid of regrets from your life. What can you do to avoid regrets? Do something. You can begin modestly. Can you name someone you owe an apology to? Do you have anything you need to share with someone? Going back to chapter 3, is there anything you'd like to attempt or learn more about? If so, contact an expert in that field and ask for assistance. By trying to live a life free of regrets, you act and choose choices that will enable you to go on.

Chapter 8: Realizing Your Objectives

Do you think you can influence how your future turns out? By visualizing our objectives, the power of positive thought empowers us to influence our reality. Using our ideas, feelings, and beliefs, we may create the life we want through manifesting. In this chapter, we will delve into the notion of manifesting and discuss practical applications.

Although it may sound like a mystical idea, the law of attraction is the foundation of manifesting. According to this law, like attracts like. We attract what we focus on, and our ideas and beliefs create our reality. As a result, we attract unfavorable events if we dwell on negative thoughts. Positive ideas, on the other hand, draw positive occurrences into our lives.

We must be certain of our desires to bring them to pass. The manifestation process requires that goals be set that are precise and unambiguous. Think about what you want to accomplish rather than what you want to avoid while you're formulating your goals. For example, make financial security your objective instead of aiming to avoid debt.

After you've established your objectives:

Pretend that they have already been accomplished.

Shut your eyes and visualize yourself in the life you've always wanted.

Use all of your senses to fully experience the sensations and emotions that come with accomplishing the goal.

Visualization is a useful technique for getting your mind and body to accept your ideal reality as genuine.

Affirmations can aid in goal manifestation in addition to visualization. Positive comments that you tell yourself every day are called affirmations. They assist in reprogramming your subconscious mind with empowering ideas and support you in maintaining goal concentration. Ensure the affirmations you employ are consistent with your aim and that they support it.

Taking inspired action is a crucial part of manifesting your goals. While affirmations and visualization are important, you also need to take action to reach your objectives. Taking inspired action is moving toward your objectives in a way that is consistent with your gut instinct and intuition. You will instinctively follow your inspiration to take the appropriate steps toward your objectives.

Finally, keeping a good outlook and remaining dedicated to your objectives is critical. Have faith that your objectives are attainable and that the universe is constantly acting in your best interests. Remain receptive to abundance and never stop appreciating all the good things in your life. Recall that every journey begins with a single step, so begin manifesting the life you desire by taking that first step right now.

To sum up, achieving your goals through manifestation requires defining your aims precisely, envisioning the outcome, utilizing affirmations, acting on inspiration, and keeping an optimistic outlook. You attract favorable events that help you reach your goals when you direct your attention and energy toward them. Have faith in the process, remain dedicated, and witness the realization of your dreams.

Putting More Fuel In Your Internal Fire

Utilizing Self-Discipline's Power

Experiencing hardship and obstacles can quickly leave one feeling helpless and disheartened. But in these exact moments, our ability to exercise self-control becomes vital to our success. The capacity to regulate oneself and stay focused in the face of adversity is known as self-discipline. It is the key that opens doors to success and keeps us moving forward in our quest for excellence.

When faced with difficult circumstances, it's critical to remember that our motivation and perseverance—rather than just outside influences—determine our success. Our capacity to exercise self-control enables us to endure and surpass any challenges.

Setting specific, meaningful goals is a key component of using self-discipline effectively. We can stay focused and on course by creating a roadmap based on our goals. These objectives serve as our compass and give us the willpower to persevere through challenging circumstances.

Furthermore, developing wholesome routines and habits is a prerequisite for self-discipline. We lay the groundwork for success by taking continuous, purposeful action. Whether it's getting up early, meditating, or working out frequently, these routines build our self-control and prepare us for any obstacle that comes our way.

Effective time management is a requirement of self-discipline, in addition to goal-setting and forming wholesome habits. Since time is a limited resource, how we use it determines how successfully we can achieve our goals. We may increase productivity and progress even in the face of difficulty by setting priorities for our work, removing distractions, and maintaining concentration on our objectives.

Moreover, a strong mentality is necessary for self-control. It is essential to cultivate a resilient and upbeat mindset that enables us to see setbacks as chances for personal development. By reinterpreting difficulties as opportunities for growth and keeping an optimistic mindset, we develop the mental toughness required to surpass any hurdle.

In conclusion, developing self-discipline is crucial for success, especially in trying circumstances. Setting specific objectives, forming wholesome routines, efficiently managing our time, and developing a positive outlook gives us the ability to never give up. We find the drive we need to stoke the fire inside and overcome any challenge we face when we practice self-control.

Creating Routines for Long-Term Motivation

It might be simple to lose motivation and think about quitting during difficult and challenging circumstances. However, developing an enduring drive is essential to overcoming these challenges and succeeding in life. This subchapter seeks to equip you with useful tactics and routines to support your motivation and keep you through difficult times.

1. Establish Specific Objectives: Begin by outlining your long-term objectives and dividing them into more manageable benchmarks.

2. Make a Routine: Make time in your daily calendar for goals-related activities like working out, practicing meditation, or reading inspirational books.

3. Embrace Positive Influences: You can significantly boost your motivation by surrounding yourself with people who share your values and objectives. To obtain inspiration and support, look for mentors, join networks offering assistance, or attend networking events.

4. Practice Self-Care: Maintaining your motivation requires attending to your physical and mental health. Prioritize things that will help you feel refreshed.

5. Celebrate Little Wins: Remaining motivated requires recognizing and appreciating all of your successes, no matter how minor. Your confidence will soar, and you will advance thanks to this encouraging feedback.

6. Accept Failure as a Learning Opportunity: Reframe failure as a worthwhile learning opportunity rather than a setback. Recognize that obstacles are an inevitable part of the path to success and seize the chance to advance and develop.

7. Visualize Your Success: Visualization can greatly enhance motivation. Every day, set aside some time to envision yourself accomplishing your objectives and the satisfying feelings and results that come with it.

8. Remain Adaptable and Flexible: The capacity to adjust to changing conditions is essential during trying times. While maintaining your final vision, be willing to modify your plans and objectives as necessary.

You will create enduring motivation by adopting these habits into your everyday routine, enabling you to overcome obstacles and succeed. Recall that inspiration is an ongoing process that calls for work and dedication rather than an isolated event. You may kindle your inner fire and never give up on your quest for a happy and prosperous life if you are committed to it and persistent enough.

Section Two

Increasing Your Optimism

A match is needed to light a candle. A tiny spark is released when the match is struck, which is used to light the candle's wick because it will die out without it. The candle wick emits more energy since it can radiate light far more distance than the match could.

Positive energy emanates from the inside, and its intensity increases with positivity. It is comparable to this in that positivity always begins tiny. Positive energy is available to you in three different ways. You may cultivate it, change your negative tension into positive thinking, or draw it into your existence. This is how you can investigate these avenues.

Creating Optimistic Energy

Your internal thoughts influence your activities on the exterior. Positive ideas are the first step towards developing positive energy. But how can you be certain you have become aware of these constructive thoughts? You have to follow your emotions as a guide.

Positive energy surrounds you when you are content, joyful, and free. This energy will motivate you to respond positively to any circumstance so that everyone you interact with will gain directly from your upbeat disposition. Being in the moment and making deliberate decisions to maintain your optimistic outlook are prerequisites for positive energy.

To cultivate positive energy, you must still your thoughts and engage in physical activities that naturally energize and uplift you. Positive energy cannot be produced by medication or other artificial therapies. These short-term, "feel good" things will lift your spirits, but they are not long-lasting, and when the first high has passed, you'll probably feel even worse. Alternatively, you can cultivate positive energy through the following methods: -

enjoying fantastic music that makes you want to dance.

Using creative writing in a book or journal can help you decompress.

Yoga and meditation

identify the blessings in each moment of your life

These easy techniques make sure that you shift your attention from negative energy, thereby reducing its strength right away, to positive energy, which puts you in the present and makes sure you can benefit from the amazing power of positivity.

Changing Anxiety into Encouragement

Anxiety, which attracts bad energy, is perhaps the biggest obstacle to our positive energy. Even when it feels like your anxiety might overcome you, it is easy to control. To be able to control your anxiety, you must identify its underlying source. By doing this, you'll be able to distinguish between how you feel about a situation and how you choose to feel about it. If you have a spider phobia, you typically react to a spider by screaming, running away, or feeling dread. You might think of them as repulsive creatures you would want to avoid since you don't understand them.

It is possible to change the strong vibrations of fear and anxiety that paralyze you into vibrations of good energy that release you and set you free. Attaining self-awareness of your thoughts and emotions might facilitate positive energy flow towards you.

For instance, consider the spiders. If you are fearful of them, attempt to identify what makes you fearful and when you start to feel nervous. Is it when they cross your mind or your vision? You can discover that what terrifies you about the spider is its meaning rather than the spider itself. You can experience less worry and more good energy by reframing this meaning into something constructive.

Drawing in Good Vibes

Attracting positive energy is intimately correlated with optimistic thoughts. The good energy you attract is shaped by the thoughts you choose to think. Here are some ideas to consider for the best outcomes: -

Positively begin your day. Decide firmly that you will have an amazing day when you roll out of bed in the morning. Go through the motions of the day acting as though you are certain that you will have a fantastic day because you believe it within yourself. Positive energy will gravitate toward you in greater measure the better you feel.

Consider the connections you have in your life. Which ones make you happy, and which ones don't? Reduce the relationships that cause you emotional distress and instead concentrate on those characterized by open communication, mutual respect, support, and trust to attract positive energy.

Accept accountability for your life and yourself. Analyze your current situation, and if there is anything you can do to improve it, take the necessary steps. Join programs, locate a support group, pick up a book—do everything that will require you to take action toward your objective. This will empower you and help you see that you are in charge of your life's course. It will also draw positive energy to you.

Look for someone you can aid when your mind overwhelms you with unfavorable ideas and makes you feel like you can't function. You will certainly feel better if you recognize that your situation is manageable and can be handled by someone whose troubles are worse than yours.

Feeling Good equals Positive Energy is a time-tested formula for positive energy.

First Chapter: Live Small, Think Small

We are frequently susceptible to small-mindedness. We succumb to our self-deceptions, anxieties, and uncertainties. We live a life of thinking little because we lose sight of what drives us.

What does it mean, then, to think tiny? According to our concept, thinking small allows the events in your environment to affect how you live. Instead of letting circumstances dictate how you spend your life, Thinking Big means being an influencer of the world and changing it.

How does this appear in real life? For illustration, suppose someone is attempting to borrow capital for their company and submits an application for a loan, only to have it denied. A little thinker would think, "I guess I'll never get a loan, but at least I tried." That implies that my business will never succeed," they say before despairing and giving up on ever realizing their goals.

Thinkers can see past challenges and concentrate on the result. "Oh, I see that my loan application was turned down. How can I get over this? As he searches for more sources of funding, he says.

We will go over each of the six parts of tiny thinking in depth. As we proceed, watch for any possible indications of tiny thinking in yourself and note which ones most resonate with you.

Component 1 of Small Thinking: Fear of the Future

It is common for us to be concerned about the future and the outcomes of unknowable events. Since we are limited in our ability to predict the future due to human limitations, it can be beneficial to understand how to evaluate risk so that our fears of possible setbacks work against us. How you respond to these feelings separates someone who healthily understands risk from someone who fears the future.

A fear of the future stems from the incapacity to perceive the positive aspects of the future, preferring to focus solely on the potential negative aspects. Fear of the future keeps you back and makes overcoming challenges and responding effectively difficult.

What does it mean, then, to be afraid of the future? It implies that when you consider your objectives, you picture calamities deterring you. You're afraid to ask for that raise by sticking out your neck. You may want to change your life significantly, but instead of working toward that goal, you cower and shrink.

Fear has a strong ability to suppress our motivation and discipline us. Fear can hold us back much more than we would like, and the more power we give it, the longer its claws remain in us, keeping us from reaching our full potential.

Take a look at these fear signs to see if fear is your main motivator:

- You've been too afraid or anxious to talk to someone.

You find yourself in a position where you must choose but cannot because you fear the outcome.

You put up with unpleasant circumstances or relationships because you don't take action.

You don't make significant life changes since you are unsure about the results.

Section Three
SUCCESSFUL PEOPLE'S HABITS

Individuals who have achieved great success share many similarities, which can be observed in their behaviors or routines. Knowing these methods could be beneficial if you wish to align yourself with your objectives. They'll help you see the seemingly insignificant things that can make a major difference in your life. Incorporating them into your way of life will ultimately lead to increased productivity. It should be understood that the behaviors you choose to maintain can either benefit or harm you. Good habits help you create a life full of accomplishments and activity, while bad habits pull you away from what you want to do.

If you put some particular behaviors that successful individuals have into practice, you have everything to gain and nothing to lose. They alter your perspective and behavior so that everything you do is consistent with your goals. Success doesn't just happen to certain people; there are learnable behaviors that can increase one's chances of success. You'll be shocked to learn that they are easy to follow and won't require much energy. They are as follows, as detailed below:

1) Control emotions: One of the best things about successful individuals is that they always make a concerted effort to keep their emotions under control by refusing to let particular circumstances or experiences dictate how they behave. They are constantly prepared to rise above the negativity and choose more worthwhile subjects for their emotions and minds to dwell on. They don't allow setbacks to cause their demise; instead, they use them as an opportunity to improve.

2) Get up early: Successful people know that getting up early is a productive habit. They know that those who wake up early are typically upbeat and vivacious. Getting up early increases one's energy levels throughout the day, enabling them to manage more tasks and ultimately boost productivity.

3) Visualize: Most successful people use visualization, essentially imagining their objectives and aspirations in their heads. It inspires you and helps you to believe in your aspirations. Visualizing these things helps you accept the idea deeply, and your actions will naturally follow your desires.

4) Planning: Without a plan, it is hard to do much in life, so business owners constantly think things through before acting. Planning will give one an idea of the best way to allocate resources and the precise steps that need to be taken. Making a plan in advance helps you to

have a general understanding of what is expected of you and what is expected of you.

5) Optimism: This is essentially what it means to be feeling and thinking positively, and it's essential to building the life you want. The truth is that optimistic people never let anything stop them from achieving their objectives because they are always willing to take chances or make sacrifices. Their heart and head work together to demonstrate that nothing is insurmountable, making them incredibly progressive.

6) Set priorities: Having priorities is another trait that many successful individuals have in common. They deal with the most crucial issues first, as they are seen to be more effective, and then the rest. By doing this, they can also prevent procrastination, which is the death of dreams.

7) Put in a lot of effort at work: Sitting about and doing nothing will not get you anywhere in

life. The purpose of life is to create, and you can only achieve this by working hard and developing the ability to make sacrifices. Nothing in life happens by itself. Thus, you must put in the effort to reach your desired destination.

Positive Thoughts And The Attraction Law

Have you ever wondered why, when you're depressed, everything feels so awful? You have the impression that everyone is targeting you unfairly. Similarly, everything around you seems exceptionally warm and pleasant while you're feeling fantastic. You have the impression that nothing in the world can depress you. You're in that pleasant persona: "Oh, you can go ahead if you're in a hurry." Let me give you a reality check: Nothing changes in the world; only your attitude does.

The Law of Attraction: What Is It?

Essentially, what we think about is something we genuinely bring about or create. It is founded on the potent idea that anything we want may be drawn into our lives through visualization techniques, positive affirmations, envisioning our objectives, expressing gratitude, and taking inspired action.

When quantum physics and the law of attraction are coupled, it becomes clear that we are a tiny particle operating in a vast universe that immediately responds to our ideas by creating our reality at a comparable frequency. The Universe works together to support us when we are focused on achieving our goals.

To make your dreams come true, the Universe responds to your thoughts at a frequency that matches your own. It just means that the Universe is reacting to our positive and negative thoughts to construct our reality, whether we are conscious of it or not. This implies that we are accountable for attracting favorable and unfavorable situations.

Focusing on what you desire instead of what you do not want is one of the most important applications of the Law of Attraction. The actual course of your life is directly influenced by the thoughts you entertain.

For example, you are likely to repeat the same patterns in the future if your thoughts are dominated by regret and guilt from the past. Conversely, you will produce more favorable future life circumstances if you can free yourself from the bonds of your traumatic past and visualize a bright future.

The Law of Attraction's greatest strength is its ability to give you control over your life. To live the life of your dreams, you take charge of your life like a remote control. Switching to a more positive idea only takes a moment to release oneself from self-limiting or negative beliefs. Because of this, the Law of Attraction allows you to use the power of your thoughts to steer your life in the right direction. The way you choose to see your future can influence it.

Have you ever wondered why those who constantly view the world from a position of "lack of" rarely manage to lead fulfilling and desired lives? Their minds are always operating from a place of shortage, which breeds more and more scarcity. Recall that the cosmos is unable to discriminate between good and evil. It has no idea what you desire or don't want. From a quantum physics perspective, it's only a matter of manifesting your thoughts by matching their frequency.

You will simply attract more situations where you lack the funds to pay your bills, travel, or enjoy life's little pleasures if you are preoccupied with ideas about never having enough money to do these things. This will cause you to reflect on your haplessness again, making it more apparent. Can you see what's going on here? It is a never-ending loop.

However, when you operate from a "plentiful" point of view, which generates even more abundance because the Universe is responding to those positive thoughts with a matching frequency, you are focusing on abundance, such as how you always have more than enough to eat, a beautiful house to live in, and a nice wardrobe of comfortable clothes.

How can you use the Law of Attraction to change your destiny in daily life now that you know what it is? Here are a few short yet quite useful suggestions.

Make Your Objectives Clear

If there's one piece of advice to make the most of the Law of Attraction, it would be to set precise goals. Try to be as specific and descriptive as you can. Don't just write that you want to launch a well-known blog in the next six months and make money from it. Make it plain. How many readers do you hope your site will have in half a year? What money will you make from the blog over the next six months?

How many followers on Facebook, Instagram, and Twitter in the next six months do you hope to gain?

What happens if you have a very precise outfit in mind before you go shopping? You might be able to give a detailed description or have a picture of it on your phone. You describe the cut, color, style, collar, sleeves, length, buttons, and every other detail to the sales assistant. The sales assistant brings a selection of precisely what you were looking for before you even realize it. You make your purchases and depart content you found just what you sought.

What might have happened if you had continued to be vague in your description? I want something to wear, but I'm unsure what I want. You would have been frustrated if the salesperson had given you many undesired options. Ultimately, you felt utterly exhausted and disappointed as you left without purchasing anything.

Substitute the description of your attire for your aspirations and the Universe for the sales assistant. Expliciting your desires makes it simpler for the Universe to grant them to you. Similarly, the Universe misinterprets your vague intentions, such as "I want to be rich soon," and reacts by bestowing upon you a sum that is not "rich" for you.

Don't concentrate or write, "I want a new house," when you desire your ideal home. Give specific details about the new residence you wish to manifest to increase your chances of doing so. What color are the curtains and walls in your home? What is the appearance of the furniture? How does the entry to the apartment or house seem from the front porch? What are the windows and doors like? What is the appearance of the upholstery? How do the hardware and electrical fittings look? Which picture frames do you have up on your walls? I take it you understand the gist? Your chances of manifesting precisely what you want to happen increase when you are as specific and descriptive as possible.

www.ingramcontent.com/pod-product-compliance
Lightning Source LLC
Chambersburg PA
CBHW052157110526
44591CB00012B/1980